THE LAST WITNESS

WAR IN HEAVEN
GERALD WELCH

THE LAST WITNESS, BOOK 00:
WAR IN HEAVEN

ISBN: 978-1-944073-56-5   **DestroyerBooks**

Cover art by Gerald Welch and Dino Agor
All other artwork by Gerald Welch

Published by Bookmason Publishing.

Edited by Donna Courtois and Laraine Richardson

Foreword by Pastor Karl Smith

THIS BOOK IS DEDICATED TO:

John Koonce,

who first opened my eyes

to the Word of God.

FOREWORD
KARL SMITH

Sometimes we only know *what* happened, but not *how* it happened. Most assuredly, we know that there was a war in heaven that was the result of Lucifer's rebellion against God. We know that one-third of God's angels joined Lucifer in his rebellion and were cast out along with their leader, now known among other things, as the Devil, or Satan.

The story you're about to read presents a fascinating account of how the war in heaven might have occurred.

Gerald Welch is a fantastic writer and story-teller. I'm not sure when we first met, but I really came to know him when I served as Pastor of the church we attended together. It was through many conversations with him that I discovered his incredible ability to think through and imagine the way things might be in the unseen realm where God and angels interact.

There is clearly a difference between the spiritual realm and the terrestrial world. Jerry has a keen understanding of this, yet presents how these two very different worlds are connected and intertwined and as he crafted this fictional story, he carefully maintained the integrity of the biblical text on which it is based. What shines through the narrative is the desire to know completely what we can now only know in bits and pieces.

With this story, he masterfully takes the bits and pieces of what is known and intertwines the possibilities of what could have been to create a story that entertains and inspires. As he tells how he imagines the war in heaven might have happened, it becomes clear that his hope is that you will be intrigued enough to want to know more about the reality behind the fiction. Jerry knows *without question* that God is real, Heaven is real and angels and other spiritual beings do in fact exist.

As I write this foreword in the summer of 2019, I reflect on something I once read from the writings of C.S. Lewis. "We can never know what might have been, but what is to come is another matter entirely"

If you're familiar with C. S. Lewis, then you know that he intertwined truth into his fictional stories. He knew that God is real and that someday each of us will stand in God's presence. As we read his stories, he clearly hoped that we would seek the God of all truth that inspired and captivated his imagination.

Such is the spirit behind this story. Be entertained as you read it, but know that the God that inspires Jerry's imagination is very much alive and well and desires for you to know Him.

Karl Smith

Pastor: FPC of Starks, LA

Treasurer: Hope Village International

Kauzone 12: 7-9

Then there was War in Heaven.

That great dragon Helel and its
rebellious third fought against
Michael and his angels.

But the third prevailed not.

Helel and its angels were cast
down to the Earth, cursed to
forever walk the world of Adam
without bodies, without hope
fearfully awaiting the
White Throne Judgment.

.

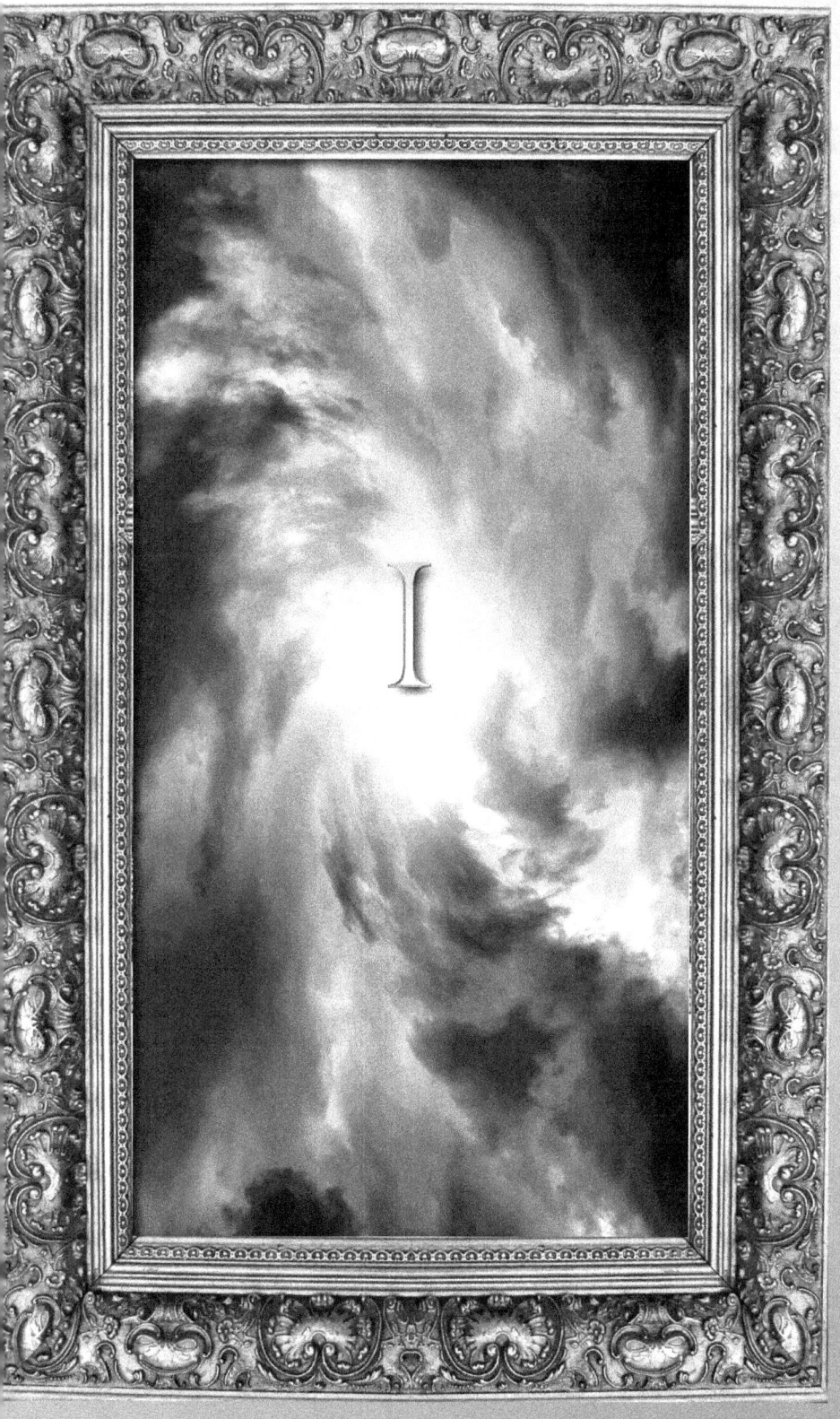

CHAPTER ONE

He was the first of all creations. Long before there was a sun or moon, even before the common physical constructs of time and space, Helel, the High Angel - the grand creation of the grand Creator - was created apart and above all else.

So powerful; so perfect, sometimes the other angels wondered why God even created them. In a universe where light did not exist, Helel radiated ethereal essence everywhere he traveled. It was an awe-inspiring sight, especially to a being like Uriel, the smallest and weakest of all the Angels.

Uriel followed and watched as Helel entered the Citadel of Creation, the infinitely large structure which housed the Angelic Host. Uriel had often wondered what existed outside the doors, but because no other Angel had a physical body, none save Helel was able to leave the Citadel. Once Uriel followed Helel in an attempt to sneak a peek at the outside world, but when the doors opened, there was only Helel.

Nothing else existed on the physical plane.

While his spiritual eyes detected far more detail than the thin spectrum available to physical eyes, sometimes Uriel would isolate just the physical elements in his vision. Everything disappeared; the other Angels, the carved columns and other enormous ornamentals of the Citadel, and even the Citadel itself.

The only thing visible was Helel and the gossamer trail of light trailing each of his steps. Uriel followed behind, basking in his misty wake.

Helel moved gracefully toward the impossibly-large chamber which housed The Great White Throne and marked *THE ETERNAL PRESENCE OF GOD*. As the towering doors were opened, the celestial tones of the Seraph's Trisagion flooded the chamber.

"Kadosh! Kadosh! Kadosh!" they cried as one. "Holy! Holy! Holy!"

Their praise rushed through the Citadel like a fresh audible mist. Helel passed the throngs of Cherubim and Ophanim, only taking time to acknowledge the first Tier Angels.

Though Uriel often marveled at the many unique features of the more powerful Angels, like Michael's Armor which could not be penetrated and Argus' flaming

Sword which could cut through anything, Helel stood above them all.

Each of Helel's twelve wings surpassed the lesser Angel's wings in power and beauty. His face was the penultimate work of perfection, gently and personally sculpted by the loving Hand of the Creator.

Helel smiled as he reached the center of the Citadel and the universe seemed to smile with him. After prostrating before He who sat upon the Great White Throne, Helel rose to the top of the Citadel.

BEHOLD!

I SHOW YOU SOMETHING NEW!

The Voice from the Throne said.

A low rumble shook the marbled walls of the Citadel - the only world the angels had ever known - as the ceiling opened. Helel motioned for the rest of the Angels to come and they followed—billions upon billions–traveling outside the Citadel for the first time.

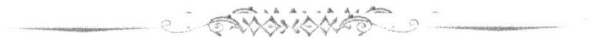

CHAPTER TWO

Helel felt great joy as he led the other Angels out of the Citadel. For their entire existence, they had only known the inside of the Citadel of Creation and now, upon exiting, each Angel manifested for the first time on the physical plane.

Helel led the Angels around the new emptiness of 'here' and 'there,' new concepts of something called 'space.' They enjoyed the feeling of movement and their faces reflected the wonder, experiencing the passing of time and traveling here and there, back and forth.

When Uriel closed his spiritual eyes, everything disappeared as before, but when he opened his newly formed physical eyes, he could not only see Helel hovering above, but the other Angels and himself as well. It was odd seeing his own hands and feet.

Uriel looked up.

The other Angels were frolicking in their newborn exuberance. Helel stood above the others, joyfully watching the Angels enjoying their newly formed physical bodies. They were soon swarming in formation throughout the new universe measuring and touching and hearing and feeling and learning.

And then came The Call.

The sound of the spiritual Trumpets that called the Angels to formation manifested itself as a compulsion and each Angel complied, moving to the solitary parcel of space where The Call led them. The Angels began to whisper amongst each other, trying to guess what was coming, but having no experience with which to guess, became silent.

The Presence surrounded them in an instant, wrapping from the inside of the assemblage to the Angels at the outer rim of the formation. The Host gathered closer, swarming to see what would be created next.

SHAMAYIM, OLAM

The Voice spoke and a soundless explosion of brilliance surrounded them. Trillions of small lights appeared from out of nowhere, filling space with tiny dots of light. It took the Angels a moment to notice that something else was newly formed at the center of their crowd. Olam, whatever it was, was dark and very large; an enormous liquid sphere covered by clouds.

HAYAH 'OWR

The Creator said and a great light appeared far away from the Angels. They flew toward the new object, which was far larger than Olam's liquid sphere. This new sphere was full of golden light and fire, like Argus' Sword. Its light illuminated Olam, showing the Angels that it was covered by clouds.

It also cast light upon a smaller object orbiting Olam that they had not noticed before. It wasn't long before the Angels could feel the warmth of the sun and they leaned toward it, bathing in its rays.

RAQIYA'

The Creator said and waves began erupting on the liquid surface of Earth. Ripples began shimmering across the planet until the water parted, revealing a surface that expanded to cover nearly one side of the world. The Angels watched in amazement as a muddy and rocky landmass appeared.

Olam had become Earth.

The Angels landed, some of them happily stamping their feet in the mud, watching as it splashed all about them.

Uriel stood amazed as the Creator introduced even more elements into the newly formed physical universe. Each new Word called more objects came into existence.

First came things called 'plants,' life forms of every

shape and size and color, rising from the very ground itself. They did not appear to be alive in any way that Uriel could see, though he could detect the universal thrumming of life in each object.

Another Word and 'creatures' spawned in the waters covering the majority of Earth. Alien-shaped figures with everything from no arms to dozens of arms sprang to life, some as small as a grain of sand and others larger than any plant existing on land, each creature was unique.

No sooner had Uriel began looking at the mélange of aquatic life than he heard sounds from above, which was odd, because the melodic squawks were not from any of his fellow Angels.

Uriel looked up to see small creatures, light and thin, flapping their wings, if they could be called such, for they did not come close to comparing with the beauty of Angelic wings; even Uriel's small wings were more majestic. The Angels applauded as the small creatures flapped around the sky.

Another Word signaled the appearance of animals on land. Like their ocean-bound counterparts, the land animals varied wildly in size and shape. Contrary to plants, the animals appeared to be alive in every way Uriel could see, but when he took a supernatural glance inside one of the animals, it was empty; there was no soul.

Uriel reflexively jerked back.

This was a paradox; the very thought of life without a soul was a mind-boggling concept!

But despite all the wonders they had seen, the Angels were not prepared for what came next.

Instead of a Word speaking the next thing into existence, the Creator Himself descended to Earth and carefully gathered some of the red mud the Angels had been playing in before.

He took a moment to fashion the ruddy clay into a small mound and began kneading the clay, forming it with His Hands.

Helel felt a curious emotion as he watched the Creator duplicate his own creation. Until this moment, Helel had been the only object in the universe personally formed by the Hands of the Creator, but this creation was not like Helel's. This being was molded solely from physical matter, in fact, the most basic substance found on Earth— dirt—but the Creator took His time to patiently craft an image that Helel and the Angels were very familiar with. The Creator was not fashioning another Angel.

The Creator was fashioning an image of Himself.

When He was finished, the Angels gasped at the likeness. Here was a form that looked like unto God Himself, but was motionless, still and without life. Then God moved over the form and breathed into its nostrils and it began to change. The clay smoothed into soft skin and the finely detailed top of its head became fine strands of hair.

Then the image moved.

Its lungs expanded with the breath of God, arching its back in birth pangs as it began breathing on its own. The Angels stepped back, not knowing what to do. This was not another God; it was an *image* of God and it was now alive. Were they expected to worship this image?

Uriel took a peek inside and was amazed. Inside the beating heart of this being was a soul, larger than any Angel's, even larger than Helel's. Uriel reflexively turned to look at Helel and for the first time in his existence saw an unpleasant look creep across Helel's face as he viewed the soul of this new being for the first time.

The image of God looked around, unaware of the celestial audience surrounding him.

ADAM

God said, identifying the new being standing before them. In that single word, the Angels understood that this new being, made in the image of God, was not God.

"Creator God, what manner of being is this?" Argus asked.

In response, Helel felt compelled to stand before the other Angels. He moved to the center of the discussion and felt all eyes watching him as he moved to stand next to the Adam.

HELEL IS A SPIRITUAL BODY THAT HOUSES THE PHYSICAL. ADAM IS A PHYSICAL BODY HOUSING THE SPIRIT.

"Won't he be too weak to survive the physical world?" Uriel's thin voice squeaked.

Other Angels turned in amazement that Uriel would dare ask a question before the other Angels.

ADAM IS MADE LOWER THAN YOU, AND IS SUBJECT TO THE DANGERS OF A PHYSICAL WORLD. BUT THE DAY WILL COME WHEN ADAM SHALL OVERCOME HIS PHYSICAL LIMITATIONS, AND ON THAT DAY, HE SHALL BE REMADE HIGHER THAN YOU.

Helel withdrew to the back of the ranks and began to think and in that moment, evil was born in the universe. It first appeared as a pinprick in Helel's soul, a tiny disagreement with the Word of the Creator. But the splinter was given place and quickly turned to envy, flourished into jealousy and then raged into hatred.

None of the other Angels noticed as the natural light emanating from Helel dimmed, but the Voice that had spoken moments earlier returned for Helel's ears only.

BE MINDFUL, MY HIGH ANGEL.
SIN HAS ENTERED YOUR HEART.

Helel bowed his head and prostrated before The Voice as he had countless times before, but this time, anger tinted his reply.

"Lord Most High, I am the first and most beautiful of your creations. How can I be made to bow before that which is lowly?"

EVERYTHING HAS ITS PLACE
AND TIME, MY HIGH ANGEL.
REPENT OF YOUR SIN
AND REJOIN THE UNITY.

"Your Will be done," Helel lied.

The words flowed so naturally, it even surprised Helel that he had so easily spoken that which was not true.

Helel returned to the other Angels, but the hate that festered in his heart began to grow.

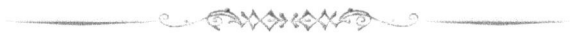

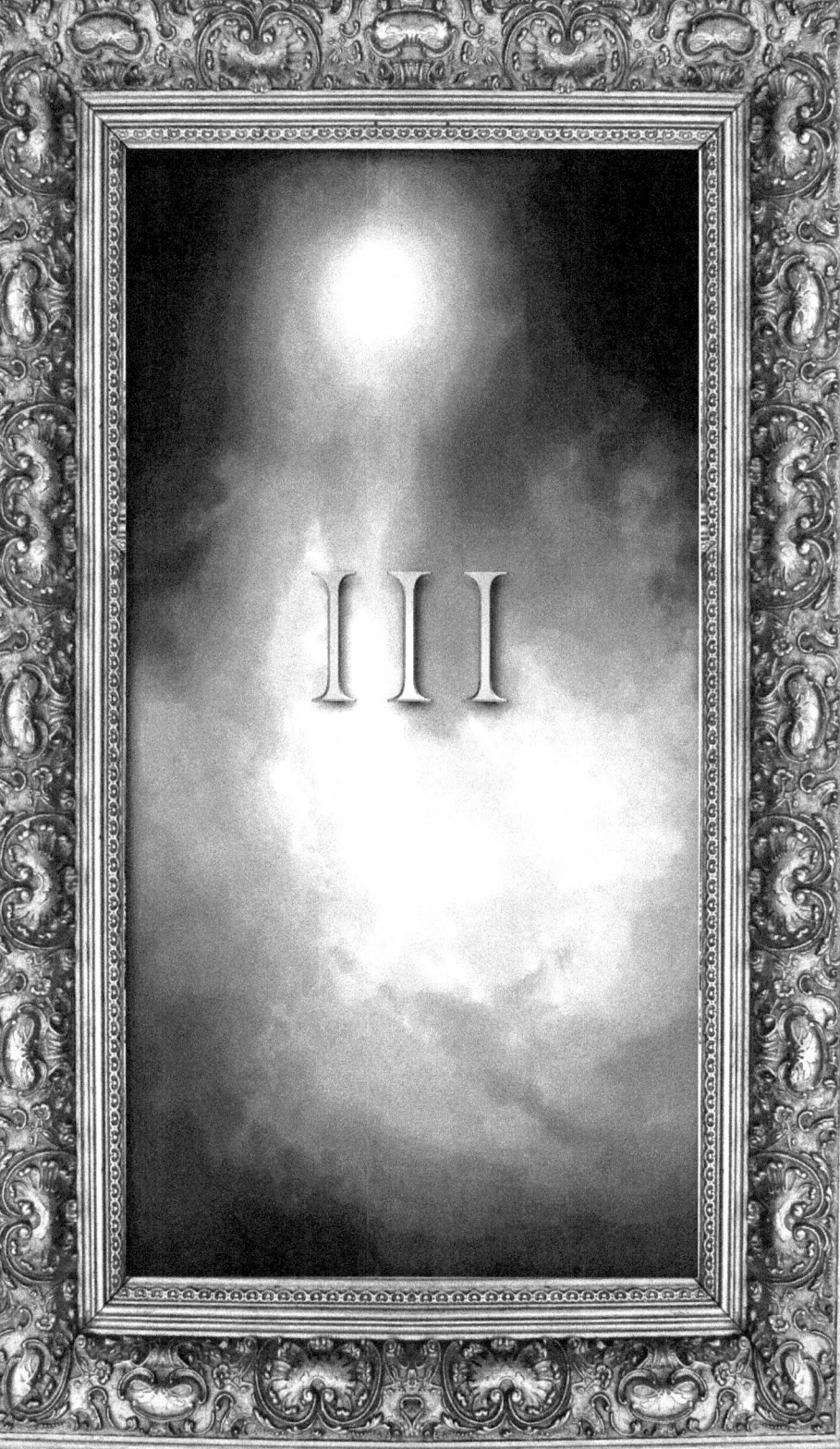

CHAPTER THREE

There had always been a clear hierarchy of things: first the Creator, then Helel, then everything else and now, Helel realized that hierarchy was no more.

He looked around creation questioning everything he saw, doubting everything he thought he once knew. Helel hovered outside the gates of the Citadel of Creation, alongside the First Tier General Argus.

Argus' Sword was the only thing in existence that rivaled Helel's brilliance and though Helel was large, he was dwarfed by Argus.

"How shall I be made to kneel before flesh?" Helel asked.

"You are the High Angel," Argus admitted. "Yet the Adam is made in the image of the Creator."

"The Adam is pale; a weak thing, simple and mortal. I shall never bow to it!"

"But it is the Creator's Will," Argus said.

Helel thought.

The dark feeling that occupied his soul had spread through his spirit and each new thought came more easily, more quickly.

"We shall rise up and kill the Adam. We shall take the Promise given by the Creator and He shall be forced to honor His Promise and make us more powerful, like unto Himself. He is bound by His Word."

The words hung in the air, stabbing Argus with their treasonous barbs, but Helel did not notice. The darkness in his heart was already solidifying.

"I do not understand," Argus said. "How do we take the Promise?"

"The Promise was that by overcoming its physical limitations, the Adam would be promoted above us. If we kill the Adam and overcome the physical limitations in its place, then we shall claim the Promise and we shall be promoted. Think…what is the only thing above us?"

Argus saw where this was headed and for the first time, felt the splinter that had festered in Helel's soul. Argus' Sword flared with his new awareness.

"Only the Creator is above us."

"I believe the Creator intends on making this Adam His equal. If He wishes to have an equal, then we shall steal the Promise and we all will be His equal! And once we are equal…"

Helel turned to study Argus' Sword, as if for the first time. Its golden flames erupted from the center of the blade, which had finely carved symbols that set it apart from all other swords.

"Your Sword. After we have been granted power, we shall go to the Citadel of Creation and use the Sword to kill the Creator."

"I…I don't know," Argus stammered.

"Then when the time comes, give the Sword to me."

Argus stood for a moment fighting with multiple levels of conflicting emotions. He understood what Helel was saying and planning, but it went against everything Argus had ever thought or known. It was too much information, too fast. Regardless, Argus knew he would never relinquish his Sword. There was something that bound him to the Sword as much as a limb or wing.

"No...I'll do it," Argus said, amazed that the words came so easily out of his mouth.

"We need to speak to the others in the Angelic Host. They will not be satisfied being placed beneath the Adam."

"I have heard questions from others. I shall bring them to you so you can explain."

"Start with the lower Tiers, but stay away from the Seraphim or Ophanim. Their Call places them too close to the Throne. Beyond all, avoid the First Tier and Metatron. They can cause problems with our plans."

Argus nodded and glided to the Citadel.

Helel watched as he left. He knew that several of the Host had questions concerning the mortals. Helel would take those honest questions and twist them to his own bidding.

It would not be long before the entire Angelic Host would belong to Helel and when they did, Helel would lead his army to the new world and destroy the Adam to take its place.

Tears of rage welled up in Helel's eyes as he thought back to the moment when the Creator formed him with His Hands and then remembered the same care given to the Adam. But while Helel was created from the fabric of nothing to be beautiful, the Adam was created to look like the Creator Himself.

Helel's jealousy raged at the thought.

"It isn't right," Helel thought, wiping tears away as the first group of Angels came with their questions.

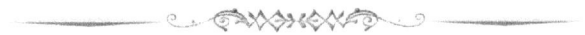

CHAPTER FOUR

The War in Heaven was the first splinter of chaos in the universe. Helel had convinced one third of the Angels to follow him and they now stood in formation at the edge of Earth's atmosphere, ready to kill the Adam below.

The remaining Host stood before Helel's legions to prevent them from breaching the sky.

Helel stood before the assembled might of Heaven a changed creature. No longer was his long, golden hair bound in the traditional manner. It now strung lazily down his back, a chaotic mess, reflecting the turbulence in his soul. Helel still shined with the Glory of Heaven, brighter than any sun or star, though his garments were now black.

All eyes watched Helel, some with caution, some with curiosity. Helel raised his hands and sealed his fate.

"Come, my fellows! Bow before me and we will overthrow He who sits on the Great White Throne! We shall create our own worlds and become our own gods!"

The Angels following Helel looked with hopeful eyes to the assemblage amassed before them, but none of the defenders budged from their stations.

Then, a small cry was heard from the midst of the Host. Though thin and weak, the accusation carried through the atmosphere.

"Blasphemer!" Uriel cried. "You shall take no more of our number!"

Helel floated down to Uriel, ignoring the combined might of the Host assembled around him, looking Uriel directly in the eye.

"You shall be the first to bow to me, little Uriel! I shall grant you a seat at my right hand and set you above all others. No longer will you be known as the weakest of all Angels. When your fellows cry the name Uriel, they shall speak it with fear! Now come...let us destroy man and take his Promise."

Uriel's tiny face knotted in fury as the entire universe seemed to hold its breath waiting for a reply. Uriel unsheathed his small sword and held it to Helel's throat.

"I bow only to One and you are not He!" Uriel said.

"Have you been to the Garden, Uriel?" Helel asked. "Now there is another Adam—a woman! They will begin multiplying and fill the world with their numbers. We must stop them while we can!"

"Holy, Holy, Holy, is the Lord God Almighty!" Uriel cried and slashed his sword.

Though not a fatal stroke, the sword drew blood.

Both sides drew swords and launched toward each another. Metatron moved between Helel and Uriel, giving the small Angel time to retreat, but Uriel advanced. Helel fell back, wiping the blood from his neck, ignoring Uriel. A small contingent of Angels blocked Uriel's advance, giving Helel time to access the situation.

Seeing only a small group of Angels defending the western sky, Helel led his strike force toward them, with Argus hidden in their midst. Helel attacked and as the first line of Angels fell, the strike force attacked the Angels behind him, creating a small opening to the last line of defense.

Argus swung his flaming Sword toward the remaining Angels, destroying them with its consuming fire. Finding a hole in the defense, Argus hurtled down to the Earth, screaming in triumph. The Angels behind him began to give chase, but Helel and the others would not allow them to follow.

Argus landed safely in the Garden.

He looked around. Despite the war thundering on the spiritual plane above, the Garden remained a peaceful and tranquil place, filled with the strangely colored objects he had seen during the creation.

From the ground, Argus could feel a cool breeze drifting through the Garden. He looked back up to where he entered to make sure no one had followed, but only saw the bright clouds that surrounded the world of the Adam like a cocoon. It did not take Argus long to find them.

The Adam creatures.

Small, pale and naked, they sat speaking to some animals. It was Argus' understanding that animals were devoid of intelligence, so why was the man speaking to them?

"This one is called a cow," The man told the woman.

"Cow!" she replied.

Argus floated down before them. They smiled upon his approach and greeted him. Neither were afraid of Argus or his flaming Sword.

"Welcome!" the man said with a soft smile.

"What are you?" The woman asked. "I have never seen one of your kind before."

The man smiled as it studied Argus.

"It is not a plant and not an animal, but you're not like us, either."

"Do you speak?" the woman asked.

Argus hesitated. He stood before the man, *the thing he was sent to kill*, but when Argus looked into its eyes, he saw the image of the Creator. And looking at his Creator, Argus lost his justification for murder.

The feelings built into the foundation of Argus' soul: love and loyalty and justice came to the surface. Argus tried to remind himself that the Adam was only animated mud.

"I am a messenger," Argus said, breaking eye contact.

"Do you bring word from the Creator?"

"My message is from the High Angel, Helel."

"What is an Angel?" the woman asked.

"We are higher beings than you, but lower than the Creator."

The Adam creatures began to bow. Seeing the image of the Creator about to kneel to him, Argus panicked and quickly stepped back.

"No! You do not bow to me!" he said.

"The Creator walks with us in the cool of the day," the woman said. "Please, stay and worship with us."

And in that moment, Argus felt it.

The spiritual realm warmed, signaling the entry of The Presence into the Garden. If Argus was going to kill them, it would have to be now.

Argus pulled his Sword back for a fatal blow, but the Adam creatures just stood there, with the same innocent smiles on their faces, wondering what he was about to do.

Argus did not know why, but he could not move. Anger flared within his scarlet armored chest.

"I was created to kill!" Argus reasoned. "This is my very Call!"

But the Sword became heavy in his hand and Argus staggered backwards as a wave of weakness passed through his body. There was something about the innocence emanating from the Adam creatures that shook his very bones...

In fear and doubt, Argus sheathed his Sword and fled before he was too weak to escape.

As he re-entered the spiritual battlefield above the Garden, Argus found that the rebellion had been crushed. Helel lay wounded at the feet of an Angel Argus had never seen before.

"You've lost!" Helel taunted as he saw Argus. "The man and woman are *dead*! The Promise will be ours and I will remember your name!"

Argus lowered his head as the remaining Angels circled him, their own bloodied swords drawn. Argus was brought to the front and thrown near Helel.

"The man yet lives...as does the woman," Argus said weakly. "I could do them no harm."

The Angelic Host cheered in victory as Helel's smile disappeared like a vapor. Helel beat back the Angels in a berserker attempt to get to Argus.

Then a burst of light silenced the battlefield and every Angel, including Helel, fell prostrate to the ground. The Creator hovered over each of the Angels, healing and reviving those who had remained faithful and passing over those who had not. The Creator lingered for just a moment over Helel.

UNWORTHY

The Voice judged.

YOU ARE NO LONGER HELEL, THE FIRSTBORN OF CREATION; YOU SHALL BE KNOWN AS LUCIFER, THE SATAN."

Lucifer felt an acidic explosion at the center of its being and arched its back in pain as The Glory was torn from it. Lucifer's wail filled the eerie fabric of the spiritual realm, causing fear in the Angels who had sided with it. All remained silent as The Presence turned its attention to the rebels and The Word was spoken.

UMBRA

The whispered Word flooded the battlefield with endless power, sweeping through each of the Angels siding with Lucifer. The change came instantly as a result of The Spoken Word Of God and they fell as their Glory was torn from each of them.

The chorus of shrieks drowned out all other sound.

That is when Argus first felt the damning effects of its choice. The Flame that had always burned with Purpose and Meaning was gone, instantly extinguished as The Word passed through it.

Argus dropped its Sword as the Holy Fire scorched its hand and Argus roared a long, desolate moan. No longer with a Call, not even an Angel, the only thing it now possessed was the insignificant purpose of self, a hollow and worthless thing.

Writhing in pain, Argus saw the blazing symbols on its Sword fade. One last spark of light and the sword clattered uselessly to the ground. Without the Holy Flame animating it, the still smoldering sword looked like any other Angel's.

For the first time, Argus was alone, separated from The Fellowship, from its Sword, from its very meaning. Argus no longer felt a connection with the millions of umbra scattered around. Each was now an independent carrier of chaos, buried in the paradoxical quagmire of choice.

Umbra.

Some would come to call them shades, while others would know them as malevolents or demons, but whatever they would be called, they were eternally damned, forever separated by a single Word from their Creator.

The Angel who stood above Lucifer, the one who

Argus could not earlier identify stepped into The Light.

It was Uriel, transformed, standing triumphantly before the defeated umbra. No longer the small Angel who had boldly stood against Lucifer, Uriel was now the size of a First Tier High Angel, holding his Sword high above his head. It was no longer the small blade that he had earlier carried; it was long and barbed and blazed brightly with the Flame that had once resided in Argus' Sword and Uriel was reborn as the Exacter of Blood.

Argus knew what was to come next, for while the Exacter of Blood is a minor office in a universe where nothing dies, the introduction of choice and war allowed death into the universe and the Call of Exacter became the most powerful of Angelic roles, holding ultimate control over every creature existing in the newly created physical plane.

Uriel's Sword flashed once and Lucifer fell dead at Argus' feet.

"How ironic," Argus thought, *"The first being to taste death was the Angel who had first called for death."*

Lucifer was merely the first to die. Argus and the rest of the umbra were killed and though their bodies were buried in the foundations of another realm, their spirits were banished to the physical world of the Adam that they so hated, bound under the physical restrictions of time and space.

Such was Lucifer's power that it regained coherence almost immediately upon landing on Earth, but the rest of the umbra lay dormant for many years.

When they finally awoke, they found that during their slumber, Lucifer had tricked the Adam creatures into being banished from the Garden, and they had reproduced into the thousands as Lucifer had warned.

Seeking guidance, the umbra gathered around Lucifer. Rage caused the edges of its very essence to vibrate.

"The Creator made a mistake by placing us on the same world as the Adam. We shall torture every one of these creatures until they deny their Creator!"

"How?" a nearby demon asked. "We have no bodies... we can't even touch them!"

Lucifer grabbed the demon by the front of its smoky frock until they were face to face.

"The Adam's soul interacts on a spiritual level and we shall use every weapon available to us: lust and envy and hatred and greed and pride and fear. And after the Adam has been removed from the protection of the Creator, we shall exterminate him from the face of this planet, take his place and steal his Promise."

Lucifer unsheathed its sword.

"And I swear, on the day I shall ascend unto Heaven and claim his promise, with this very sword...I shall kill the Creator!"

Lucifer held the sword high. Argus recognized its former sword by the faint markings that ran the length of the blade. The sword was held aloft, like Argus used to hold it when it was full of Glory, but now it was a simple, dull metal.

Argus looked solemnly at its former ally. It was clear that Lucifer would never trust him again.

Lucifer returned Argus' look with a smile, but not the same smile they shared while in the Citadel. It was bitter and as jagged as barbed wire.

Making sure Argus was watching, Lucifer thrust the sword into the air again, and it ignited into black flames.

Then Lucifer brought the umbra together, separating them into their new dominions and tiers. Argus was forced into a third tier and sent to a different realm, never to return.

New commands were given, new assignments made, but as the centuries turned into millennia, the goal remained the destruction of man and overthrow of Heaven.

The War itself never ended, but the battlefield moved. …to Earth.

That sound behind you; is that a sword being drawn?

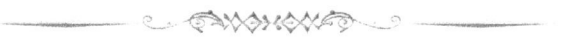

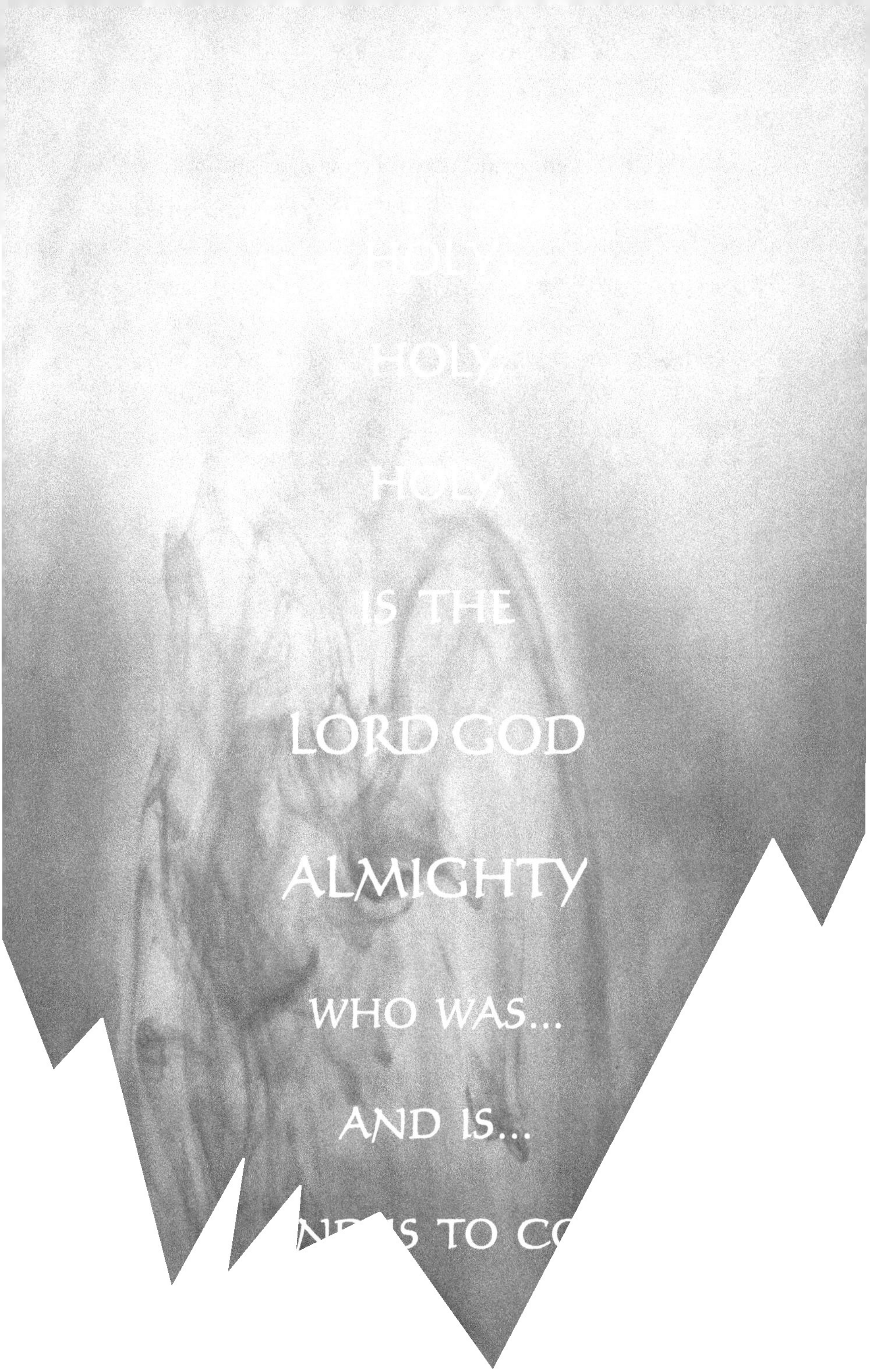

HOLY,

HOLY,

HOLY,

IS THE

LORD GOD

ALMIGHTY

WHO WAS...

AND IS...

AND IS TO CO

If you enjoyed War in Heaven, you'll *love*
the other books in *THE LAST WITNESS* series!

*"Jerry Welch's 'The Last Witness' is a startling, exciting
novel -- of ideas and action from a young writer and artist
of unmistakable talent and energy. I can't recommend it
highly enough."* -- WARREN MURPHY, two-time Edgar
award winner and creator of The Destroyer series

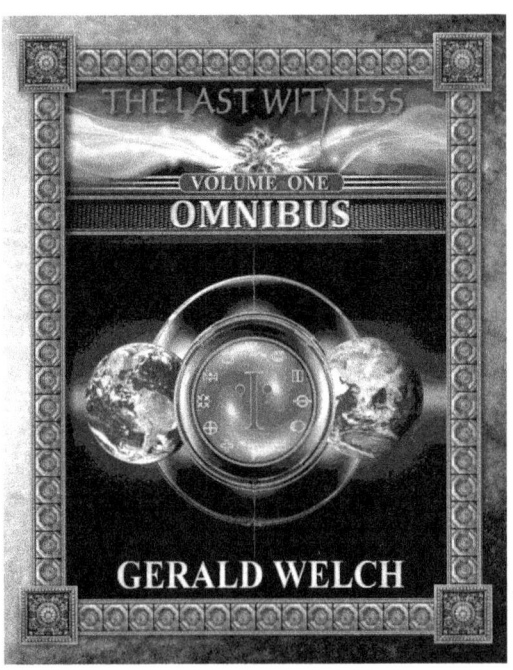

Start with the 416-page *collectible hardback* edition!
It includes War in Heaven, the first two books in the
series as well as a detailed encyclopedia that features
character entries, maps and a whole lot more!

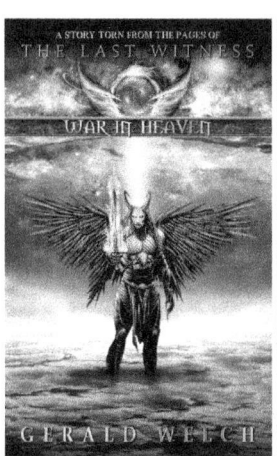
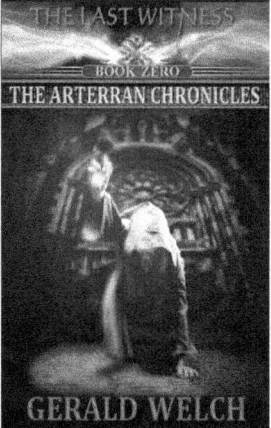

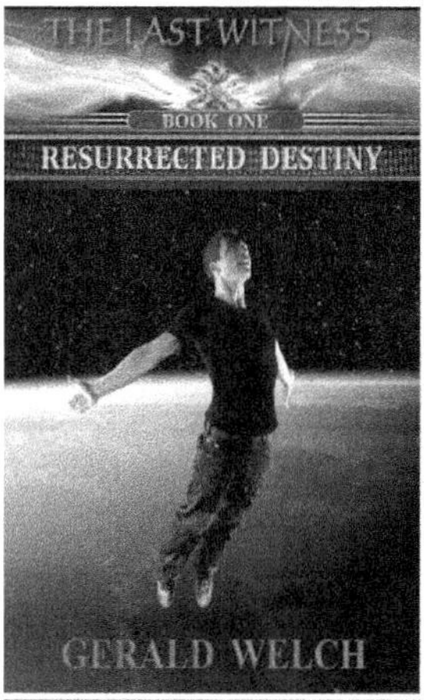

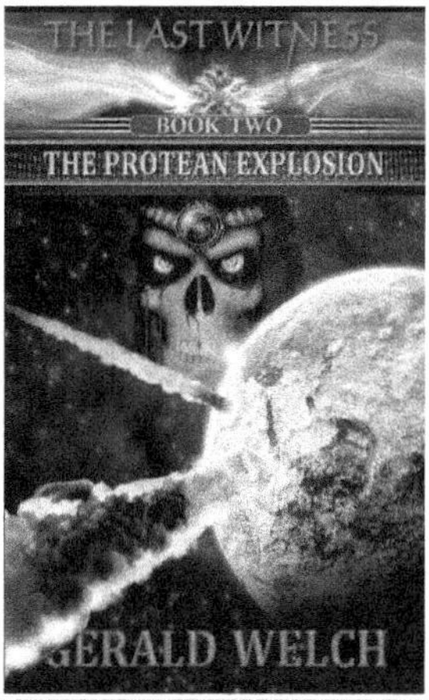

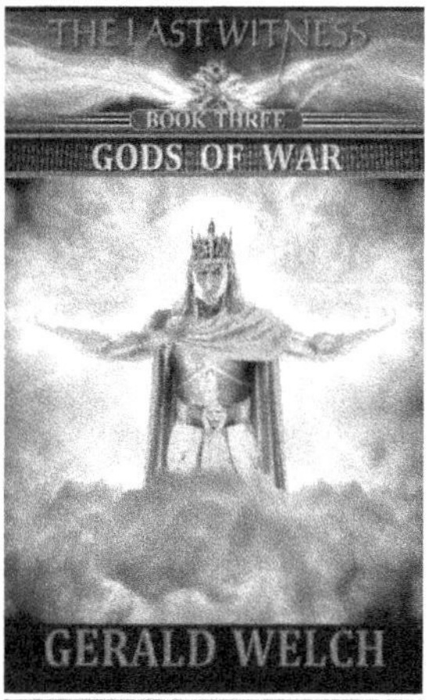

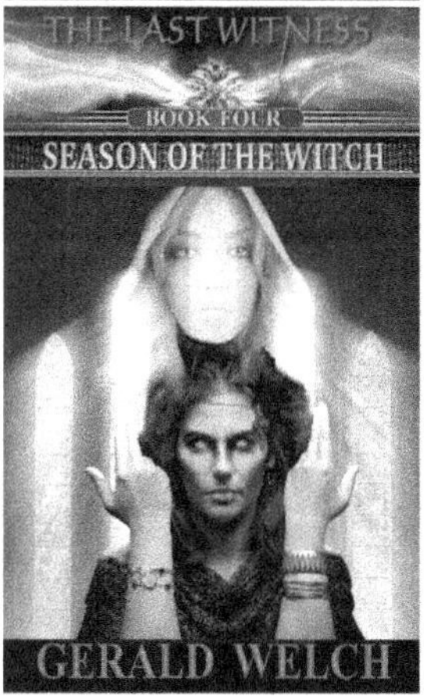

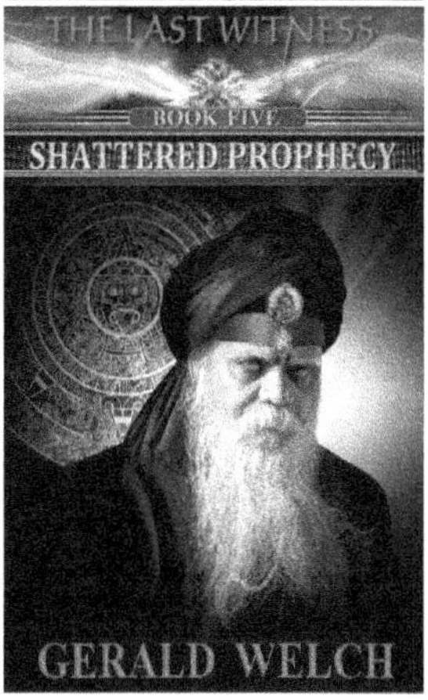

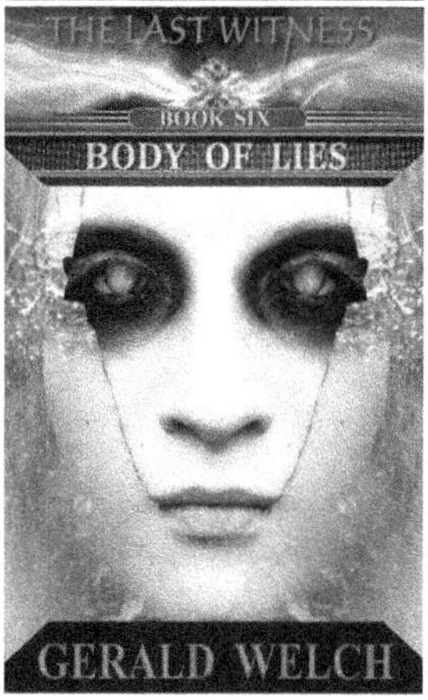

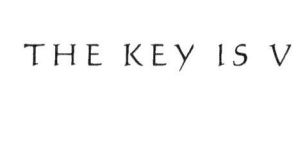

THE KEY IS V

www.ingramcontent.com/pod-product-compliance
Lightning Source LLC
Chambersburg PA
CBHW051334220526
45468CB00004B/1642